The Oracle to Freedom

Sizzond Zadore

Copyright Jon Whistler

http://www.LightPulsations.com

First Published in Australia in 1998 by
Light Pulsations Ionic Healing Pty Ltd.

Reprinted in 2016 – LightPulsations.com

All rights reserved. No part of this publication may be reproduced, stored in a retrieval system, or transmitted in any form or by any means, electronic, mechanical, photocopying, recording or otherwise, without the prior permission of the copyright owners

ISBN 0996744177.

Contents

The Opening……………………………………….. 5
Focus……………………………..………………... 9
The Beginning…………………………………… 15
Consulting the Oracle…………………………. 19
The Moment……………………………………... 23
Earth Body Connection………………………. 29
Surrender………………………………………… 35
Guilt and Forgiveness…………………..……… 41
Self Obsession…………………………………… 47
Symphony of Life………………...……………. 53
Generation………………………………………. 59
Freedom…………………………………………. 67
Fear………………………………………………. 75
Illusion of the Astrals………………………..... 81
Healing the Earth……………………………… 87
Balanced Ego………………...…………………. 93

The Oracle to Freedom

The Opening

I am your Oracle of inspiration and revelation. I have always been with you to encourage, illuminate and lead you back to Me, because I am the Oracle of Light - One Light, which is you. Listen, while I encourage your mind and feelings to dwell on the beauty of the Light, to complete your journey home to the realm of Light, which you never left.

There is no mystery, because all mystery lies in the Astral Illusion, which has been woven around your Personality which is forgetfulness. There was a time when you drank from the waters of the river Lethe, in Hades, the home of the Astral Lords, and forgot who and what you are. Time and again, you have returned to the Earth in a cloud of forgetfulness and illusion, seeking to express control and mastery over the Earth and all that exists in its energies, and this prevents your return to Light.

These Oracle Cards will create a resonance within your consciousness, stimulating those frequencies which will lead you back to Me - One Light in consciousness.

Every step you take will immerse your mind and feelings in the messages which the cards impart, and will free and burn up the negative thoughts and emotions of your life recurrences. This in turn, will accelerate development of Being.

All Light and Consciousness is directed by you to the Earth through your Personality from Essence. The book, One Light, opened the way for you to empower the Earth. Following this book, the Transmissions revealed in Enter The Vortex as One

The Oracle to Freedom

Light, gave you the keys that unlock those memories which have been imprisoned in your being following your denial of Light.

The Oracle Cards when used every day will merge your consciousness with the Vortex of Light and Healing (VOLAH) releasing Light, Healing and Oneness in your consciousness.

Once you have experienced the intensity of the Light, the glamor of the Astral Illusion will fade into obscurity. There is no limbo, because you are not stranded between dimensions. The Astrals can offer you nothing because you are free from their control. Freedom is yours to take. Grasp it NOW! Move into the multi-dimensional frequencies that constitute your wholeness. Daily listen you ME as I guide you in the ever expanding frequencies released, urging you to replace those old habits, which were Astrally motivated, designed to harmonize all consciousness with One Light.

Do not be attracted to any groups that are formed to study Zadore's Transmissions, because you share your Light with others by moving into the center of your being, because it exists only there, and here you will experience the freedom which the Transmissions reveal. Groups produce hierarchical levels for those Personalities locked in the Astral Illusion. There are no leaders in Light, because the Light doesn't lead or control. Only the god created by the Astrals behaves in such a Manner. It is this god that grants you favors, loves you, punishes you and expects you to worship it. Know that the Light Is, and your Light on all dimensions also Is.

The Oracle Cards are structured in such a way as to move your energies into the Vortex of Light and Healing where you will experience complete attunement with all you are. Third-dimensional groups hold your consciousness in bondage fragmenting it.

The Oracle to Freedom

You do not have to give anything away when seeking the Light except the Illusion in which your Personality is immersed. There is no reality in the Illusion, nothing to gain and nothing to lose, because it doesn't exist. You are the Light that you have always been, so stop focusing on the Illusion, because within the Light there is no Illusion.

'The inspirations and meditations in this book in conjunction with the Cards will open your consciousness to the Truth and Light. There are some rituals you are encouraged to follow, which help you attune with your inner Light. However, in this in this work, every day, as with an onion, you will peel back the layers of negativity, and enter the silence of your being which reveals its Light and purpose for you, because this is the purpose of the Oracle Cards.

As you remove these layers of negativity you will cleanse and transform your consciousness. Do not constantly recite affirmations because they are only hollow words that have no depth or meaning for your inner consciousness, and are based on intellectual concepts that are devoid of any feeling and true desire. Affirmations have no effect over the behavioral patterns you have developed in the Illusion.

The Astrals use affirmations to create fear and prevent you from rediscovering your freedom. They are powerless and can't stop your unfoldment, because they have power only over those individuals who surrender their energies to them.

Through their Illusion, the Astrals broadcast negative energies to influence the mass consciousness of humanity, seeking to block the Earth from receiving the Light needed for its ascension and freedom from Astral domination. You stand at the forefront of change, and as you change, so too will the consciousness of others change...

Yes! You are important.

Focus

How long have you searched to experience the ultimate freedom? Have you sought enlightenment through the religious experience, mystical writings, esoteric groups, Eastern masters or the old Astral mystery schools? What have they taught you that led you to freedom? You have followed their teachings, waited, worked and when you did not attain the desired enlightenment, you were you had to wait for another life, another time, because when you are ready then the Master will appear. Then you will be invited to join a hierarchy of mystical masters and learn how to control the feelings and minds of others in the group. This control is done through the use of magic and deception, and leads you into greater darkness and despair.

At your present state of transformation you are tired of following the rules and rituals that lead nowhere, except to bind you in service of their cause, one which denies personal freedom and demands blind faith to follow their agenda, all under the guise of Mastership. What constitutes a Master? Is it someone that holds themselves to be greater in power and consciousness than others, and able to sway them in following the Astral consciousness and Illusion.

How often have you heard this statement, "there are those, like you, who have learned the laws of life, and are now masters who no longer need to have an earth-body, and work on another dimension and plan and structure humanity's future". These ascended masters are the Astral Lords who contrive to drain from humanity their Light energies for their own existence and have no care for the welfare of anyone, including their Entities.

However the Astrals have underestimated the depth of human consciousness, which is linked to the Light through Essence, reviving the memory of its true state in Being, and in turn dispels the Astral Illusion in their consciousness.

You don't need these masters because all knowledge exists within, all you have to do is break the seal on your book of life and open your consciousness to the fullness of your being.

Don't look backwards, because the past has nothing to offer; seek not a future based on the time frame of the Illusion, because there is no future, no past, only now in the Eternal Moment.

The Oracle Cards will help you rediscover the One Light. They will inspire, free and lead you to be One Light, the ultimate freedom. Desire and become this.

What is it you must remember? Your Light Essence, and unless you become aware of this, and continue to focus your energies in this direction, you will not experience One Light.

You have to become aware that your body is important in your work for transformation; however, without a body and consciousness in this dimension you cannot reach any transformation in consciousness. In the Transmissions you have been taught that you are not your body. But in the Illusion you believe that your body is you. However, because you are so identified with your body, this causes you to become separate from what is the real you, your Light Essence. The Personality utilizes the body to live through the senses that are dominated by the negative forces of the Astral Illusion, which asserts that when the body dies you experience the desired freedom. This is a lie designed to hold you asleep to the real state of your Light and consciousness.

This false and confused understanding of the body is the greatest illusion ever forced on human consciousness. In the silence of your being you should question what this means, and then you will understand your original purpose. Was it not to give your light to the Earth, and to open the Earth's consciousness beyond its limitation in this dimension? The only way to experience One Light is to be fully conscious of your body and its real need. This may appear simple however, it will lead you to experience freedom.

Do you ever express true awareness of your body? What do you consider yourself to be? Your Personality is so engrossed in the Astral Illusion that you act out your life without any thought or feeling for the Earth's needs or its body which you indiscriminately destroy.

For example, when a situation angers you, such as when you are driving in traffic and upset by the negligence of another motorist. You brake and instantly give vent to your anger, directed to that driver. Your anger is spontaneous and without thought. After composing yourself you drive on and begin inner talking directed against the driver.

Your subsequent feelings and thoughts are based on justifying your behavior, building up negative energies that flood your cells and nervous system. You don't see the mechanicalness of your action, and the harm you are causing to the Earth's consciousness.

Have you ever tried to stop this negative flow, and then observe how your body is feeling and reacting to this stress? If not, then it is time you did, because you will then begin to open your consciousness to perceive the frequencies that underlie your body and the Earths consciousness. If you do this you will see how you are destroying the Earth's consciousness. Anger is an Astral frequency which walls out the reception of Light, so is it any wonder that your body becomes sick and worn out prematurely?

Being self- centered and Astrally controlled, you have little awareness of your body's importance for the Earth, because by moving your Personality away from serving the Earth, you are also moving away from One Light.

There are no educational systems that can teach you how to understand your body's relationship with the Earth. It has nothing to do with the illusory concept of worshiping the "body beautiful", in its outer form. Before you can attune with your body's consciousness, you have to feel and know that it has a separate consciousness from your Personality and its self-image, because its consciousness is one with the consciousness of the Earth, and the Earth's Personality.

When you are immersed in the worldly aspects of your live and enjoying all the sense related activities of the Illusion, you are completely unaware of your body's true feeling. You are unconscious of the involuntary movements, reflexes and constrictions which are affecting it inwardly and outwardly.

Wake up and become aware now of your body's reactions to all these desires and wants. Practice methods that will alter your Personality's delight in the Illusion and become aware of what you are doing, which is denying the Earth of its Light.

Your journey is complete when you remember your purpose for being here. If you are honest you will see that you are only focusing on your body when you are in fear, which arises when you reach that stage where tour health deteriorates and become ill and die. Daily through your selfishness you create

The Oracle to Freedom

conditions that harm your body, and on a larger scale, humanity, in its grab for power and control thoughtlessly destroys the Earth.

When the health of your body reaches that state of degeneration it is a reflection of how little Light you have given it, and how much you Personality loves the Illusion. You will find that your reactions are often the result of imitation of the attitudes and feelings passed down through many past generations.

These attitudes and feelings are misconceptions that are built in human consciousness which are designed to hold your Personality captive in the Astral Illusion. It is time to question the validity of your attitudes, emotions, morals and beliefs that are designed to move human consciousness into the Astral Illusion and destroy all freedom to be.

The Transmissions break down these false concepts by changing the way you thank and feel. Use the Oracle Cards every day and begin to destroy your false beliefs and move consciousness into the Light.

All disease that develop in the body come from the negative emotions that your Personality, and this causes separation of your outer consciousness from your body's consciousness, as well as the separation from One Light.

In the Illusion you have been told your body is a hindrance to your experiencing the truth within. It is seen as being heavy and dense, chaining your higher consciousness to matter. For many, the inner Light is seen as being something indefinable, something that grows out of the repetitive life events and experiences. You are told that for inner growth to occur, you have to suffer all the indignities imposed on the body; that you are debased and imprisoned in the body; and this debasement reflects the weakness of the flesh; and the body is aligned to the dark forces inherent in Nature.

This twisted reality holds the Personality in bondage to the Astral Illusion, even though the Personality struggles to become free of its body identification. The Personality feel alone is the cause of all the pain and suffering it endures, preventing it from having the freedom to enjoy the fruits of the senses. This denial only moves the Personality deeper into darkness.

Turn away from all the misconceptions that have driven you further from the Light. Look lovingly at the true nature of your body, because it is your greatest asset that holds the key for your advancement in Light.

You begin to become free when you become aware of the importance your body is for inner unfoldment, where you begin to become free of stress, illusion and restlessness. You don't have to travel the world, seek fame and power, or make a change in your employment, all you have to do is change your way of thinking and feeling, and experience how you feel in your body, and how your body responds to this feeling.

The way is clear, because the Oracle Cards will direct your consciousness in the direction of Light that will move that Light into the body and the Earth. You will no longer experience the pain of the Illusion, but the joy of Light and oneness in all.

The Beginning

You should use this book and cards in conjunction with the book, "Enter the Vortex as One Light", and then this Oracle will blend your consciousness with the energies of the VOLAH, and you will harmonize the frequencies of your outer consciousness with your Light being.

As you study and practice the exercises of the Oracle, you will sense that you are moving closer to your Light Essence, and that it is moving closer to you.. But neither is occurring because you are already one. However, the varying dimensions of your mind, sets your consciousness apart from experiencing your oneness in Light. The different levels of your mind are arbitrary, because different words are used to express the same state. You hear a reference to the unconscious or the sub- conscious mind, the subjective mind, objective mind and the body's mind, and so on, but what is it within you that is the inner power of your One Light? It is certainly none of these, because they are all different frequencies of the third dimensional memory patterns. Only by attuning with the Oracle Cards will you achieve separation from the different aspects of mind and matter, and discover your oneness in Light.

In Transmission Seven, Body Consciousness, reference was made to the unconscious urges generated through group participation in sporting events and the like, where group emotion stimulates old body memories, which, in turn, feed an energy flow, causing those involved to behave as if of one mind, in an uncontrolled destructive manner.

Unconscious behavior occurs daily in your life and in the lives

The Oracle to Freedom

of others, making you continually act from your unconscious habits. Take the time to sit quietly and review your day, and see how often you acted in a conscious positive manner. See how often your actions, words and thought patterns have followed a habitual expression. You are asleep to your inner nature, because only when you move into an alpha or meditative state will you begin to experience your freedom from habitual expression.

Subconscious expression is closely aligned to your Personality. There has been much written about the power of the subconscious mind that has a powerful effect on our lives. From birth you have programmed your subconscious to act in a particular way, or else allowed others to program you.

This is done through the persuasion of others, either directly or indirectly as well as by the Astral Illusion in the form of role models.

The subconscious is easily influenced by internal and external desires which causes the subconscious mind to be an active expression of your Personality, and because the subconscious is connected with everyone, this is virtually called the collective subconscious. When you desire to bring about a particular result in your life, you do this by applying a positive suggestion to your subconscious. Any result is always dependent on the clarity and intensity of the desire, and what desires these changes is your Personality. Understanding this you will see that your life is controlled by the Astral Illusion through Personality.

In your journey to Light to reach your purpose, you need to stimulate your desire with renewed energy every day. The Oracle Cards will do this for you. The Cards will keep you focused, which will break down your habitual behavior and expand your consciousness allowing you to achieve greater attunement with Light Essence and Being.

The inner mind or subconscious is the real mind of Personality, and when unconscious behavior occurs at sporting events, it is the result of old memories locked into the body that surface in an uncontrolled outburst. At times you simultaneously express influences that have their seat in the Personality and body, and you vacillate from one extreme to the other, blown in the wind from one place to another, one desire to another.

Your movement into the VOLAH occurs at a rapid pace when you daily consult the Oracle Cards.

The Oracles pictorially awaken in your mind images that release past memories, not only from the present life experiences, but from other deep seated memories in your sub conscious. The sub conscious mind dwells in the realm of imagination, because this is where its true power exists, and because of this image creation, the Astral Lords were able to seduce the Personality with their Illusion.

The sub conscious mind doesn't experience time, because it acts and dwells in the ever present. Like everything beyond the Third-dimension it is timeless!

The sub conscious mind uses the body to manifest what it images, and doesn't care whether the manifestation is beneficial or harmful for the wellbeing of the body.

However, it uses the earth-body to manifest what it images, and doesn't care whether the manifestation is beneficial or harmful to the wellbeing of the earth-body.

At present, many of the Personality's images are illusion bound and don't manifest harmoniously with the earth frequencies and Light.

On an individual basis, when destructive images are created, the body can experience such problems as stomach ulcers, high blood pressure, overtaxed nervous system, limiting the body's function.

Through the desires of the Personality, negative projected images

The Oracle to Freedom

create destructive influences for the Earth and its bodies.

We know that beyond these influences there is something that watches, desires change and suffers from being ignored. Often it speaks out, but it is never heard. It questions the Personality's actions to little avail.

It's your true being, the One Light in you that reacts and desires these Transmissions, which leads the Personality to image the desires of Light and Love. This is your true Oracle, one that breaks your negativity and frees your imprisoned consciousness.

This is your beginning where you become the being that you are, a being that is awake and vibrant in Light. Your Oracle will lead you through the Cards images to freedom.

Consulting the Oracle

The Inward Movement...

You are beginning your daily journey to freedom, and you will select a particular time every day when you will attune with the Oracle. You are developing a new habit, one of Light.

Always select the same place to move into your alpha state of relaxation. It is your special place attune with the Oracle. It's safe from the intrusion of the negative frequencies of the Astral Illusion.

Read aloud the "Release". When you have finished reading sit quietly for fifteen minutes and allow your consciousness to be free.

Then:
Select your Oracle Card.

Allow the imagery on the card to enter your consciousness. Close your eyes - and feel, see and listen.

Choose the same time and place every day and practice the release.

The Release...

I am relaxed - I feel comfortable - I shall not go to sleep

The Oracle to Freedom

during this release. (Take a deep breath)

I am inhaling the energy of light and peace into every cell of my body.

(Exhale and see in your consciousness an electric-blue balloon and all the air leaving it; watch as it softens.)

Like the balloon, with every outward my body releases all its tensions - like the balloon it becomes limp and relaxed.

I feel all my toes becoming soft and relaxed - they feel limp. My feet are soft like a sponge - the more I relax the softer they become. I feel this softness moving up my legs to my knees - and from there to my hips. Both legs feel deeply relaxed - there is no muscle or nerve tension - they are soft and completely relaxed.

I am aware of all my fingers - they are discharging all the tension from my arms. I see the tension moving out from my fingers like rays of energy. As I breathe, the release of pent up energy increases, and my arms become soft and relaxed as the last rays of tension leave my fingers. Now my arms and legs are completely relaxed and soft.

Feel completely limp in my arms and legs - they begin to draw all the tension from my back and shoulder muscles. I am moving into a deeper state of relaxation - my whole body is soft - limp - relaxed.

There is a feeling of quietness in my legs and arms. With each breath this quietness and peace is moving throughout all my body - soothing - penetrating - quieting.

I feel completely relaxed. In this quietness I see a pure white light emanating from every cell in my body - it radiates out in all directions. It forms an oval light around

The Oracle to Freedom

me - an auric egg of pure white light. I am encompassed in light. I AM LIGHT - I AM ONE LIGHT.

Sit quietly in the light of your being and allow your light to reach out to all Light.

When you are ready select your Oracle Card, and read the Oracle Transmission. Allow the words to enter deep into your consciousness. Focus your attention on the selected card and allow the imagery to enter your consciousness. Sit quietly - don't expect anything - because there is nothing to expect.

Just allow the imagery and feelings to draw inwardly to your inner being.

This isn't a time for meditation, because the Oracle Release will affect your consciousness for twenty four hours. It works continuously, releasing old patterns, both in your waking and sleep time. It allows your Light to break through your illusionary consciousness allowing you to become free in Light.

Repeat this Release using the same card for as long as you draw it. your inner Oracle will guide you.

Consult the Oracle every day!

Editor's Note:

In the following Transmissions Zadore uses the terms Ego and Personality in a particular way. Often writers use Ego and Personality as having the same meaning, and often interchangeably with the word Soul.

Ego is a lens that acts between the inner Light Essence and the Personality. As such the ego breaks down the Light frequencies so that they can manifest at the conscious level of the third-dimension.

Personality is erroneously thought by most people to be their self. Personality is not present at birth and develops as the consciousness of the baby is filled with the outer sensual experiences, influence and outer knowledge of the world. When the Personality desires the sensual passions of the world it effectively blocks the flow of the higher consciousness from the Light Essence.

The Moment Card

The Moment Card

The Oracle to Freedom

You have drawn the Moment Card, a card that your true being seeks in order to encourage you to enter the stillness in Light, and help you to stop desiring all the outward experiences of the Astral Illusion.

Humanity places a major emphasis, and a dependence, on the concept of time, because the Astral Illusion is powered by time, and it is the illusion of time that regiments and controls the thoughts and behavior of human existence. Time reduces your creative abilities, because you often feel there is never enough time to complete all the different tasks you want to complete. However, most of your desires are embedded in the Astral Illusion and not within you.

Often you here people remark that time is not an illusion, because time is a measurable factor based on the relationship of the Earth and Sun, of day and night, as well as the annual movement called a year. If you were to move your consciousness to another part of the Galaxy, time as you perceive it on Earth has no meaning, and an irrelevant in your consciousness.

What humanity chooses to represent as time is a frequency pattern of the energizing process occurring between the Sun and Earth. This has no meaning to the consciousness of the Sun and Earth. Having no meaning in the Sun and Earths consciousness, it doesn't change the Earths energy level whether the rotation frequency is ten or a billion times. How do you count the number of inward and outward breaths you take every minute of the day? You take this for granted, and so you should, because it's a frequency of the moment and has no other subtle meaning. And the Earth cares little for the demands of humanity's time, which is only a cycle of movement.

To reinforce the value of time in your life you could say that

The Oracle to Freedom

you remember past events such as the things you did yesterday, or even a year ago. Because this appears in your consciousness as representing a progression through time, you attach this memory to a specific year. Does attaching a memory to a number, accepted by you as representing a period where the Earth moved around the Sun actually create an existence in time?

Because the Astral Illusion represents that time is something that is linked to a specific number, by removing that number concept from your consciousness, you can "see" there is no such thing as time. The number attributes to the day or month of the event occurred in your consciousness and not a year ago but NOW! Your memory or re-experience of something occurs now in the Moment of your being, serving to provide you with a meaning of it now.

Whatever you have experienced at any time in your life has no meaning for anyone else, unless they were involved. You don't exist in someone else's consciousness. Your experiences are a part of your consciousness, serving as an attempt to express your Light, and do not exist in time.

As such, the future doesn't exist, because the future is the past. What is expected, planned and desired will eventually come to pass, and these planned events are thought to be the past, because the effort used to create or image a condition or event ceases when the moment of realization is experienced. If you think, "I began this twelve years ago", you are still using numbers to confuse the moment. There is no past or future, only the present moment, and to live fully n the Moment of your being, you have to live in your Light.

Life is the Moment of Being, one that encompasses many experiences, and is always focused on giving Light to the Earth.

The Oracle to Freedom

Everything you have ever thought, done or lived represents the Moment of Truth within what is real, the timelessness of Being.

You create images which are unconsciously experienced as different events, but in reality, are all leading you to express the Moment, which is timeless, the One Light which is YOU. Here there is nothing more, no past or future, only the changelessness of all consciousness which is Light, something that desires nothing, because it is everything, requiring no plans, goals, images or progression, because It exists in the perfection of Itself.

Every day you run one way or another trying to find and discover the secret of success, immortality, love, possessions and power. In fact, you think this will make you happy and free. When you attain those desires they lose their glamor and appeal, and you become more dissatisfied and begin to seek other goals. This is living in the Illusion, because it can't lead you to greater freedom, and by creating goals in the Illusion, you become further separated from the Light which is YOU.

The message this Card imparts is that you stand quietly and live in the Moment of your Light, which is represented by the star whines brightly, giving its Light and energy freely to enrich the Earth. It symbolizes the Light within you.

The multi-coloured rainbow is like the many frequencies that represent the different experiences you flow through from recurrent lives.

Like the tree, you are encouraged to stand in your beauty and Light, allowing all to flow from the truth of your Self. You are beautiful, and everything around you is beautiful. In response to the Light's energies, the rainbow colors the sky and all lives as an harmonious one.

Stand silent in your being - as the tree stands - serene and expressing its nature. It desires nothing and sends forth its beauty, giving all it receives through its leaves, from the Sun to the Earth. Its form expresses its true nature.

To the tree the star doesn't appear to be separate from its consciousness, because it stands in its light. Stand in your Light and feel the power of the Moment. As your Personality becomes submissive to the flow of Light you will radiate from your body the beauty and peace of all. No matter what you do, whether you have a skilled profession or not, this same Light will flow through and you express it daily in your efforts and service for the Earth. You lose nothing by living in the Moment, nothing except fear and anxiety and other repressive feelings of the Astral Illusion.

Cast aside any occupation that is destructive to the Earth and Life, because if you continue to be employed in occupations that create goods and services that destroy life on Earth, you cut off your consciousness from your Light. You can't change something that is destructive by being involved in its production. Disconnect yourself from those occupations, because without your support they will eventually cease to exist.

By expressing the good, like the beautiful tree, you will live in the Moment of creation and One Light. In this Moment there is no stress, no desire, only joy and love.

To live in the Moment recite the following before you begin your daily attunement period.

Meditation...

My life is a beautiful experience, and each day I am more

The Oracle to Freedom

aware of the beauty and goodness in all others.

In living my life, I express beauty and Light, which radiates throughout and from my body. I love this body, I love the Earth that gave me this body.

To this Moment I bring a new image of myself, one that expresses only those desires to live in the Light, knowing that this too will touch and change others who, in turn, will express their Light and beauty.

This reflects every thought I have about myself and others. I see myself fulfilling this Moment of my life, because I live in the Moment of being Eternal.

In conjunction with this card it is recommended you study Transmission Twenty in "Enter the Vortex as One Light". Apply the transmission daily as you work through this card's message.

Earth Body Connection

Earth Body Connection Card

The Oracle to Freedom

Often you've been told that YOU, the Light of your being, are not your body. It's important for you to recognize the need for your connection with your Earth-body, because it fulfils the expansion of Light in your consciousness.

You would not possess the dimensional light you have were it not for your dimensional-body, whether it is of the earth or another planet in the galaxy or universe.

For many millennia, Zadore has been connected with the star body of Sizzond, who, in turn, has been connected to an earth-body through the ego. There is always the need for the higher consciousness to move through the dimensions utilizing a form relative to the frequencies of the particular dimension. In the Third-dimension and on this planet the particular form is the Earth's form which is the human body, and this body reflects the higher consciousness for the Earth.

All that is in All, Being, extends itself throughout its creation, and by reflection or mirroring, Light, Life and Love, it becomes aware of its own existence in its creation.

You too need a body connection to reflect the beauty and love of your being on this dimension.

The words, unconditional love, Light, the god light within, are only words attempting to describe the feeling that flows through the Earth-body, allowing it to reflect the Love and Light not only back to Being, but also to everyone you connect with through that body.

Beauty exists in everything and this card seeks to fulfil your response to giving and receiving, because as you recognize the Love and Light within others, so too will you recognize it in yourself, and will be able to love the light of your being.

Earth bodies are the expression of its consciousness. You are drawn to the body because it represents the power to shine

The Oracle to Freedom

outwardly YOUR Light, which is the I Am.

For this to occur within the body, the Personality must turn from the Illusion and allow the fullness of your Light that is projected from a higher dimension to fill the Earth's consciousness. Cast aside the Astral Illusion and allow your Personality to fulfil its destiny - reflecting Light and consciousness to the Earth.

Now, touch your body with the unselfish Light and Love of your being. Feel the consciousness of the earth Feel the earth's consciousness and become aware of the earth's beauty, because once you touch the earth, your earth body, you radiate all love into the third-dimension, although you are unaware that you are doing that.

You have drawn this card because it is time for you to touch the earth and experience the expansive consciousness of the planet.

Move your feeling into this card's meaning. You are the Light, pure and shining, and as you reach down through the ethers, you touch the earth's body, and make the connection. Understand and learn the depths of your body, because it contains all the secrets, the life and consciousness of the earth.

Your body is the total experience of the earth, because your body's consciousness has grown out of the earth. It stands as a mighty oak tree, its roots stretching deep into the earth's body, drawing up the crystal energies of the planet/ It expresses all consciousness, the plants, sea creatures, land animals and birds, because the body is the flower of the earth, opening its petals to the Light, sending forth perfumes and color for all to bathe in its beauty.

This is your body and you will begin to experience its beauty as you allow this light to bathe every cell. How little you know about the earth-body. You don't even know what it really looks like, because you are only aware of it through the feelings it expresses, as well as its reflection in a mirror. You know very little about your body, and your only concerns are knowing how to stop the pain you inflict on it, and how to express the sensual reactions it produces in response to the Personality's wants.

Reach down through your Ego and touch the earth with the creations light, and the earth will respond to this kiss of love as it rises to empower itself and radiate Light to the distant parts of the Universe.

All the earth-bodies are like many planets in the Universe, bathing in the Star light. There are about seven billion human bodies all sharing in the Eternal Light. You can touch these seven billion bodies when you radiate your Light through your body connection, because as you touch others, you increase their Light, where Light begets Light, and this connection creates a massive out-flow of light across the planet.

All your body projects and radiates this Light, because are the animals, the reptiles, fish, birds, insects, trees plants and all the elements. Your body is the Earth, and the Earth is beautiful.

Express the beauty of your Light and Love for the earth, now, as you live in the moment of the Earth's consciousness. Express all that is positive for the earth as you daily develop, through your work and expression, those conditions that are conducive to the upliftment and reception of Light for the Earth.

Drawing this card calls forth within your being the true connection with Life. Often you have asked, "Why am I here, and what is the purpose of this short life"? Religionists are unable to answer this question, because they are so imbedded in the Astral Illusion, they can't discern the Light that flows toward them.

The Oracle to Freedom

Your purpose is to connect and experience the beauty of Light as it expresses itself and through itself, and you are that Light.

A body dies and another is born, and it is the massive sway of birth and death that represents the changing consciousness of the Earth. Within each small body the same cycle occurs as cells are cast aside when new ones are made. All life is renewable, all is becoming.

What is constant in this Dimension is the flow of unconditional Light and Love. This flow is unchangeable and doesn't follow the Earth's cycle and its organisms, which renew their existence, something that is necessary, because the body strives to become Light, which flows to and through it.

The Earth Body Connection Card will open your memory pathways to understanding the meaning of the life expression you NOW participate in.

Meditate daily on the symbolism of this card, and allow your Light and love to touch others.

Meditation...

I express unconditional Love and Light as I radiate it into the creation. I love this Light which is ME. In the deepest sanctuary of my Essence I know I am the Light.

I know that all other beings are composed of the same Light as I am, and that their bodies are of the Earth. This being so, we are all connected to the Earth and the Universe, and, in this, we live, stand and have our being.

The Oracle to Freedom

In all others I recognize the same Light that is within me. I love all others, and, in so doing, I love my Self.

My Love, my Light, enriches my days as well as the lives of those around me.

My creative expression is increased through living in the Light of my being, and this amplifies, enriches and develops all others who I contact every day, because my Light opens the Light in others to the Earth's Light.

It frees those I love, allowing them to expand their Light and Love so they can reach their own fulfilment, making them free.

I AM - Now and Forever

The Oracle to Freedom

Surrender

Surrender Card

The Oracle to Freedom

What does drawing this card mean for you? Sit quietly and ponder its significance in your life, because this is a message of freedom - but freedom from what?

Listen and your One Light in consciousness will answer this and many other questions that enslave your mind. Where there appear to be no answers, just questions, you are moving through the Illusory flow of Personality.

Don't question. Because questioning alone won't reveal the truth of your being. Questions always demand answers, and those answers won't necessarily match what's asked.

You see, Beloved Light Being, much of your search for knowledge and understanding is directed to your Personality, and your Personality is centered in the Illusion, and not in One Light. All your answers are tainted by the teachings flowing from the Astral Lords.

"What must I surrender?" I hear you ask. It's the desire to know all, and the willfulness to take control of your life, its direction, and your desire to express your Personality through the Earth-body.

The purpose of Ego is to bring consciousness and Light into the Third-dimension. However, as you realize Ego has no personal expression on this or any dimension, because it's only a lens that focuses and directs information to and from the Earth through its bodies.

Ego is created as a frequency to allow the flow of One Light to the Earth and its bodies, and this Light gives outward expression in the body as unconditional Love. The Astrals, through their Illusion, appealed to the Personality's vanity by offering them power and wealth, knowing they would turn from Light and serve the Illusion. In so doing, the Personality became the Astral Puppet... and are still blinded by the

The Oracle to Freedom

baubles, believing they are now gods in the world.

By turning from One Light, Personality collectively lessens the impact of unconditional love for the Earth, and replaced it with the force of the Astrals, which is based on power, control and destruction of the Earth.

This darkens your consciousness; a consciousness that now believes it experiences all the joy and suffering the Earth-body expects.

As the lyricist wrote, "What the World needs now is love sweet love!"

You have become attached to and tainted by the desire for power and control that only under extremely stressful circumstances, you turn to One Light and desire, and your Personality then turns in that direction.

What must you surrender? It's all desire to express a personal selfish attitude, one that seeks to dominate, control and be remembered... as one who lives forever. All desire must be surrendered, as you allow the Light to express Itself. In fact, surrender is allowing all action to express oneself in harmony with the energies of Light.

Following conception, the Earth-body develops in the womb, and the mother's participation in the Astral Illusion ultimately sets the memory patterns within the body's cells. These patterns are already determined by the sperm and ovum, however, the parent's emotions now begin to inflict more changes on the developing fetus.

At the time of birth, your consciousness flows through the birth vortex, and as the new Earth-body passes through the birth canal, there is a connection created with the Light Essence, and consciousness flows into the Third-dimension, and a wonderful event occurs.

The Oracle to Freedom

His new body is full of Light and Love, which shines forth for all to see. Everyone associated with the new born child responds to this vibrant out-flow, and at that moment, responds to, and re- discovers their own Love and Light. It's as if your Light is as a candle flaming in your heart, warming your emotional out-flow. The love and joy expressed by the new born makes this happen, warming your consciousness, producing peace and joy in every fiber of your being.

Now you understand, because you feel a quickening in your whole being, as the candle flame burns in your breast. Soon you forget, lose contact, and fall asleep in the habits you've developed over the years. Try to rekindle these feelings and allow the flame to brighten, so that each day you will experience the warmth of unconditional love in your life. Then you will become a beacon of Light, which you were when you too were born. It's no different, because you still have the same body and Essence that you has at your birth, only now your consciousness, locked in the Astral Illusion no longer expresses unconditional love. This now is the moment when you regain the original state of your being.

Everything of the Earth awaits the Light and consciousness of Self to express its One Light through the creation.

Everything moves toward Light, and so too does the Earth's energies, expressing the power, light and beauty when they reflect their being in the Sun's Light.

The Earth's energies surrender to the life and light flowing through them, animating them, expecting nothing, receiving all, giving all unconditionally. That my Beloved One Light Being is what's love is all about, a cycle of giving and expressing the essence of Being.

The Oracle to Freedom

The beautiful butterfly hatches from its cocoon and moves freely through the air, the Sun outlining its colors as it gives freely the love and expression from the creativity of its being. It lives to continuously express the cycle of Light, and when it lays its eggs, it continues the progression of the Light and Love of its species.

A child's mother, with a rosy hue on her cheeks, also shines outwardly, blooming, as she receives the love and light radiating from her baby, and in turn, radiates her own light and love for all to receive.

To surrender is to re-discover that Light and Love which, is you. Now your Personality becomes passive, and is replaced by the active flow of Light, which begins to destroy the Astral Illusion.

The surrender of Personality is not a moment filled with remorse, because you don't have to atone for past mistakes, which belong to the Astral Illusion. Atonement is an illusory action that keeps your consciousness dwelling in the past, breast-beating and seeking forgiveness.

This is not necessary for you now, because by surrendering your Personality to One Light, you have nothing to atone, because you ARE!

Having surrendered your Personality you live in the purity of Light and Love. You expect nothing, judge no one, or expect any particular behavior from others, because you are once more Light and Love, as you were when you were a baby, only now you are conscious of the Light and Love.

However, in this moment, you expand your Light and Love for the earth, a being preparing for its rebirth in the same Light and Love.

Meditation...

The Oracle to Freedom

Relax and become quiet.

Move your feelings deep within the beauty and symbology of this card, because it asks you to remember.

It compels you to surrender, to surrender your Personality's fascination with the Astral Illusion, and all desire for that darkens the expression of your One Light.

"I'm relaxed and release all those experiences of the past, because I know there's no need to seek forgiveness from those who I've hurt, and, in turn, I don't need to forgive others who hurt me. I know there's no hurt or pain in Light, because all hurt and pain are the illusory frequencies flowing through the Personality.

"The One Light that flows through my refocused Personality wipes clean all the negative, harmful and destructive thoughts and actions ever made by me… they fade into insignificance.

"I fully realize the past effects of many life recurrences, and I am now free… free to be One Light. I completely accept the truth of my being.

"Living every moment in One Light, I give love and help to everyone… unconditionally and unencumbered. I have fulfilled my nature, and given my body the Love and Light, which it will carry deep into the Earth's heart… because I AM ONE LIGHT!"

Guilt and Forgivness

Guilt and Forgiveness Card

The Oracle to Freedom

Have you ever felt guilty feelings during this life experience? How often have you sought forgiveness for your wrongs?

You've drawn this Card because it's the moment in your consciousness where you have to confront these issues, and when you do, you will draw closer to One Light.

Throughout the history of human consciousness, the feelings or frequencies of guilt and forgiveness have been deeply embedded in the memory patterns of the human body, affecting conscious expression. Often what is called conscience is not the whisperings from your higher nature, rather it's the stirring of fear, the fear of retribution, and that your actions, when discovered, will be revealed for all to see.

Guilt is a frequency which has its roots in the Astral Illusion, and from here it flows through Personality into all Earth-bodies consciousness.

On a personal level, what does guilt mean to you? Is it a pleasant experience?

All Astral Illusional experiences manifest at the level of Personality. Often you are encouraged by the Personality to act in such a way that you may appear to be more intelligent, physically stronger, or even more capable than you actually are. Usually this leads to being competitive, and if another person is the winner, then you feel hurt and inferior, and will go great lengths to put down and undermine the person, who you feel cheated you. Eventually your behavior becomes obvious to others and your credibility is destroyed. Now your Personality makes you feel guilty, and you blame yourself, which leads to feelings of inferiority.

Should your actions reach the point where you physically or mentally injure the other person; you feel guilt every time you

The Oracle to Freedom

hear something about that person, or when you see them. Inwardly you think they blame you, and actually, they DO!

Often you seek forgiveness for what you did with an act of repentance, hoping you will be released from your sense of guilt. Does it?

Even if you your apology is accepted, whenever you think of that person, or when you talk to them, inwardly you ask yourself, "Did they really mean it?" In this way your Personality controls your feelings.

The concepts of guilt and forgiveness have been served up to humanity more often than any other part of the Astral Illusion. Effectively this has distanced your living as One Light.

Guilt is used as a means of control, and it is a powerful negative tool, which when understood is used by everyone. Governments use it to prevent anyone from asserting their right to free speech; religions use guilt as sin, and this binds the sinner to the church, which has the sole power of forgiveness; and every human being uses guilt as the means to assert their advantage over others. Parents use it to control their children use it to control the parents; and people use guilt to gain advantage over others in the workplace. Everyone moans about their suffering from their feelings of guilt and often seeks forgiveness to alleviate their suffering. That, in itself, demonstrates the depth guilt reaches in our consciousness.

Drawing this card suggests this is the moment for you to unveil your true feelings, because you often act in such a way where you are unconscious of why you behave in a particular way. Often you automatically burst forth in a fit of rage, hurting someone you love, and at the same time they feel guilt believing they have somehow provoked you.

The Oracle to Freedom

Such behavior usually stems from your childhood, where you experienced feelings of insecurity, which have been forced deep into your unconscious, such as being unloved and not wanted, not being smart or good enough. Later these feelings of insecurity are expressed as resentment toward one or both parents. You blame them because you believe they are responsible for the hurt you feel now.

However, mostly they are unaware they did anything to hurt you so deeply, because they raised you the same way their parents raised them, and they feel no resentment toward their parents. Who should you blame? Your parents, grand-parents, great-grand-parents or great-great-grand-parents? Are you any more special than all of them?

However, you believe now that it is all bound up with not being loved and not parenting, where your parents failed to support your efforts in coping with life that they never praised you when you expected it, and now this blame has turned to rage and violence. You feel pity and seek to make them realize their guilt.

Guilt and forgiveness go hand in hand, where one is seen as freeing you from the other. Initially the Astrals introduced the concept of forgiveness in the Illusion as a way of anchoring the Personality in the Illusion, because even while the Personality sinned, there was a way out, which is to seek forgiveness from an illusion based God, and depending which God was sinned against, so too did the forgiveness ensue determined by the penance ordered. In some instances forgiveness requires a mediator who has the authority to act on behalf of the God to forgive these trespasses. In other instances there is a sacrifice required such as killing a beast, and worst of all is sacrificing a child to appease the God's wrath. There are as many ways of

The Oracle to Freedom

dealing with guilt as there are religious sects that have their existence through the ignorance taught through the Illusion.

How can anything like this take away the wrong and guilt experienced? And how can you live with a God that demands penance for forgiveness?

The symbology of this card is joining together, where you reach out through time and space to touch the hand of One Light, which is guiltless, because fear doesn't exist in Light. As the wave curls and rolls onto the sand, and reforms itself, so too will you cleanse your consciousness of all guilt, which has prevented your movement in Light. The hands express that everyone can be like this with each other when they live in the Light - the human hands reaching to one another, as you reach for One Light.

Stop feeling guilty, because there is no guilt in One Light, so there is no more need to seek forgiveness. Allow the Light to shine, as the Sun shines on the ocean water, purely and freely.

Step aside from your Personality and inwardly look deeply at those people whom you feel guilt with. Look past their Personality and see the magnificence of their being. Love surpasses all Astral desires, especially those based on guilt and forgiveness. Give this love to your parents. Are you any wiser or better than them? If they are no longer living then allow this feeling to develop in your inner Light and let your love flow to them, which will eliminate the need for words of forgiveness. Your Light hasn't been hurt.

Lastly, move aside from your Personality and all its Astral attachments and experience the magnificence of your Self, because once you touch the beauty of Light you will no longer experience fear and guilt, and everyone will respond to your Light and Love.

As long as you wallow in your feelings of guilt you will see guilt reflected in others. Reach out to them with your One Light.

Meditation...

"I realize that it is only my Personality that makes me experience guilt for my past actions. I don't feel comfortable dwelling on those events where I caused others to suffer, and I don't feel comfortable blaming others for my present feelings. I don't seek their forgiveness, because the One Light within me has done no wrong, it is pure and perfect... It's ME.

"I'm now feeling my Essence with a vital awareness that comes from One Light. It's a powerful force in my life.

"I realize there are no permanent obstacles in my life, only temporary ones which will be overcome by my daily expression of unconditional love flowing through me from One Light.

"I see the flow of my Light moving and cleansing my Personality of all the negative effects of the Astral Illusion... because everything fades into obscurity as my Light moves out to those who I once thought hurt me... and those who I feel I've hurt.

"We are all one in this Light, and this Light is for the Earth and its Ascension."

Self Obsession

Self Obsession Card

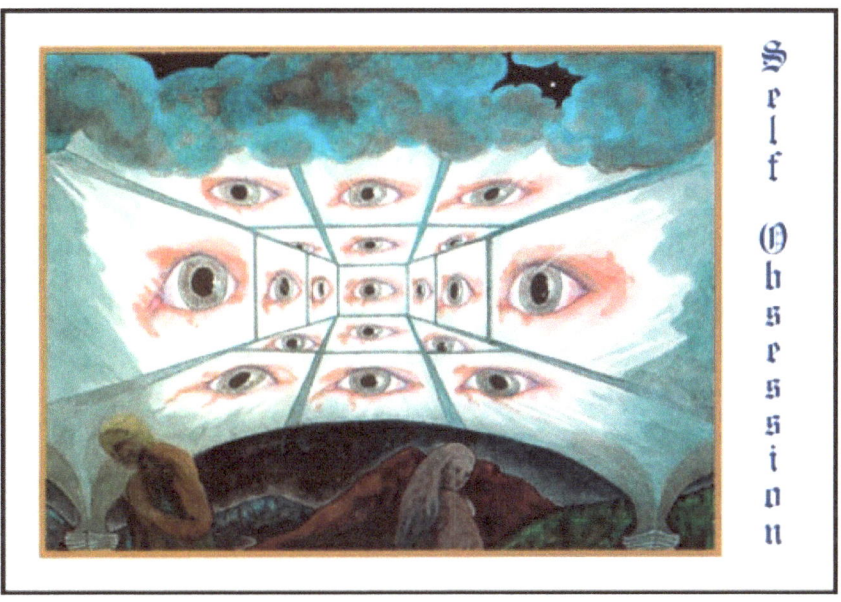

Gradually the Personality turned its gaze away from Essence and caused darkness to engulf the Earth and its consciousness.

Now the Human Personality became obsessed with its own importance, beauty and self-importance and projected this image to other Earth bodies. This produced an ambivalent relationship, because in some ways the Personality became so identified with its body that it thought other forms were reflective of its own self, and following this identification and attachment, it believed that its body is something that restricts its freedom in life.

The Oracle to Freedom

After focusing on the frequencies flowing from the Astral Illusion, the Personality began to believe it was God-like, and all other earth-bodies were dependent on it for all that was... in as much as it expresses the shameless illusory desires into the Earth-body frequencies.

But the self-obsessed Personalities in the Earth's bodies looked at each other, each reflecting its own desire for power and control, and human consciousness, the Earth's consciousness, became darkened and starved of the Light so needed and desired.

The Personality dwelt in its own illusion, which was developed by the Astral Lords, because they manipulated the sensual desires of the Personality, and at the same time manipulated the Earth's desires.

This reflects the world's consciousness where you work and live, because it's a constant manipulation, which the Personality seeks to dominate as it reflects its will through the Earth-bodies eyes, shamelessly seeking petty sensual rewards, always looking outwards and not seeing the Light that abounds all dimensions of the creation.

Begin to understand what this means to your daily life, because whether you live in a rich or poor country, humanity will always live in degraded circumstances, often with insufficient food to sustain their life energy and existence.

The Astral Entities who live in countries called the First World use their greed to deny people in other less fortunate countries the same standard of life they enjoy., they've made provision in the Third World countries for the entities of their own kind to take all aid and deny others the necessities of life and freedom.

However, it is little better in the so-called First World

countries, where the majority live in fear that their so-called rights may be denied them, and also they won't enjoy the freedom they think they possess.

The Personality's self-obsession is self-imposed in that the Personality desires power and domination over all it perceives, and this power and domination was a promise by the Astral Lords, a covenant made long ago.

This card, which you've drawn, reminds you of the Illusion, because the Personality has one eye that gazes outwards, and all the earth-bodies act as mirrors that reflect thousands of eyes. Which is the Personality's true eye, and doesn't every reflection mirror the same eye?

Here you see and understand the apparent diversity all Personalities as they reflect their image through many different earth-bodies, and the Personality becomes obsessed with the diversity of for,, and accepts this diversity as reality.

As the Personality turned its gaze away from the Light, which flowed through it to the Earth, then the Earth too was unable to receive the full Light of Self, but only what radiated from the Sun as well as the stars in the universe.

The captured Personality could only move only sensual desire and fear into the highest morphogenetic pattern of the Earth, the human body, which in turn, began to direct its negative frequencies toward all other forms on the earth, reducing the manifestation of Light.

In denying the Light on Earth, the human Personalities attacked and destroyed many other forms considered as lesser beings. Animals that couldn't be tamed or domesticated were slaughtered to the point of extinction. With the destruction of forests, humanity has methodically reduced the Earth's communication with the other planets in the solar system.

The Oracle to Freedom

But these negative behavior patterns are not limited to the so-called lesser forms, but are inflicted on their own kind. In the cities there are thousands of malnourished children, homeless people, and refugees. Daily innocent people are attacked and murdered with little regret by the perpetrator.

Bombs wipe out villages, air pollution create breathing difficulties and disease, and killer viruses manufactured in labs are released on the unsuspecting population. How often do you throw your hands in the air exclaiming? "What can I do? Has the world gone mad"?

You are responsible for everything that happens in the world, because you remain asleep to the real power that exists within your being, and continue to serve the desires of the Astrals in their Illusion. You are not blameless, and once you realize that, you have to change your state of being, taking responsibility and turn away from desiring all the sensual pleasures and negativity of the world, and seek to live in the Light of your Essence, which you are.

How much longer do you have to suffer before you will make a change? Even when you are faced with life threatening experiences such as a terminal illness, or whether your loved ones are attacked and killed, is it only then that you direct your inner thoughts to seek guidance and help, to begin to deny the darkness and suffering? And when things don't work out, you begin to blame your god for all this? And if you recover from all this agony, do you quickly fall asleep once more in the Astral Illusion?

Your Personality has many reflected eyes that look outward, seeking ways and means to keep control over your earth-body, and there are so many earth-bodies that constantly feed on the Personality for sensation, wants, greed and power.

The Oracle to Freedom

To "Love one another as I have loved you", is to love your body, the Earth, and in turn everyone will begin to experience Light and Love now.

Tenderly seek to renew the Earth…, tenderly seek to renew your body by only seeking the Light, which flows through the Personality to YOU.

Stop looking at others, and surrender to the Light, and then you'll experience the Light Being you are, and also the Earth will have the same experience.

Meditation…

In drawing this card I'm moving my Personality into the awareness of ending its gaze at all negative illusory propaganda that denies the Earth Light.

Every moment in consciousness I seek to express the power, beauty and love which the Astral Illusion denies me.

As I turn away from the degrading influences which my Personality is entangled, I feel the warmth of Love which knows no bounds, because I'm that Love and Light.

I submit to, and surrender all consciousness to the Light and Love which the Personality has denied the Earth through my earth-body.

As I become filled with this Light everything around me becomes affected by this Light, and all is beautiful, and I'm beautiful.

The Oracle to Freedom

I'm lifted into the realms of Light and taken away from all fear and desire, because the Light of my being is all Light… and everyone shares in this experience.

The Oracle to Freedom

Symphony of Life

Symphony of Life Card

Attunement and Purpose

How often have you yearned for quietness and stillness within your consciousness, a freedom from the flow of thoughts and desires passing into your Third-dimensional consciousness?

Often you take hold of some idea, a desire to do something that gives you pleasure and a sense of achievement following it through to its conclusion. However, when the end is reached, sometimes there is a bit of a let down; somehow the culmination of the achievement has lost its glamor. Desires last no longer than an hour before they are replaced by another bauble, because you're like a baby who reaches out to take every new object dangled before its eyes.

Being driven by your senses, you flit from one objective to another without any purpose other than satisfying a fleeting desire, to end your state of boredom, because the Astral Illusion has little to offer that's of any depth.

There is only one thing that awaits your discovery, which is the mystery of your Being, and how often do you really search for this fulfilment?

"I know there's something special for me to do here!" You think, and you trust that it will be important, something which others will look up to you with acclaim.

Know that it's your Personality and the Astral Illusion which works together to draw your desires in that direction.

This card reveals that your life is enacted through a prism, reflecting various life experiences, where in some of these experiences you were powerful, great, evil, pompous, and more often than not, unknown. You are one of billions of people who believe that this NOW is their special time, a time where they

The Oracle to Freedom

can be brilliant and wealthy and have all they desire. However, in essence this is your special time which means you have to stand aside from all previous experiences, because all your life experiences are One Life, One Light, One Being and every past experience is a segment in the curve of expression as you move your consciousness through the Astral Illusion, becoming aware of how pointless its been, and now desiring to become ONE.

You've planned and detailed your frequency to function in the Third-dimension, moving through a series of earth-bodies, and you are tied to the oneness of your being. This plan is like a great symphony which you composed and it won't end until the last movement is complete and you are whole.

Are you now an important being? Are you well known? Does your photo regularly appear in the newspaper or on television? Are you one of the beautiful people? If so, what does this experience mean to you, and where is it in your symphony?

Are you searching through the trash cans looking for food? Do you sit on the sidewalk with a begging bowl? Or do you look out the back window of your "Mercedes" at everyone you consider less fortunate and don't share your level of importance?

No matter what position you hold in life you're enacting your symphony, and just how you play the instrument through your Personality, is how the sounds move through this dimension.

"Your focus on the Third-dimension may last for ten earth years or ninety, and even after your body dies your consciousness remains at its present level of consciousness, soon to return to complete the symphony. When, during this life-experience, you raise your consciousness to a higher level than what you started then you come one step closer to completing your symphony.

The Oracle to Freedom

Constantly you allow your Ego to act as a prism which separates the Light into many colors, which distorts the frequencies and leads you on the path away from One Light and deeper into Illusion." (Enter the Vortex as One Light)

This card depicts your separation and fragmentation into many lives colored by the prism. Remember that it's your higher consciousness which composed the music for your experience… its experience.

Your life has intervals, movements, high and lows, and your consciousness flows through them as they express the essence and purpose of your higher consciousness until the last experience reaches its predestined completion. You're unaware of its direction and often mistake some of the rhythmic changes as indications that your life is out of control, because you're unaware of who composed the music and its intent.

"Often your life appears to be a mix of uncompleted desires. What you think you want and need is often thwarted, and in your frustration you suffer and blame outside influences, such as governments, family, friends, nature and God for your misfortune. You're told by the Astral Illusion that you must take charge of your life and raise yourself above such disastrous happenings, and then you won't be buffeted by these attacks on your security.

"Sometimes the composition is short, and for others long and demanding, but it can't be altered until it's played out. There's no pause or stop button, because it must continue until it reaches its conclusion.

"There's only one composition which your higher consciousness has composed, and it's divided into segments, and is played fully over many life experiences. However, often you allow your Personality and the Astral Illusion to pervert

The Oracle to Freedom

the flow by interference. This is due to your sleep state of consciousness which creates a repetition of the same events making it necessary for you to return to allow the completion, and then in one last experience you play the whole symphony and become one in Light.

"You've never been greater than what you are now, because all other life experiences have led to now. When you move into the frequency of consciousness which expresses your purpose through your higher consciousness, you experience the harmony of now. You will no longer be buffeted by disruptive energies, but you will follow your experience in a prepared way." (Enter the Vortex as One Light)

The words from Enter the Vortex as One Light capture the essence of this card, which is one of great importance for your daily movement into the Vortex. It doesn't matter whether you're rich or poor, starving or gluttonous, because you're playing your symphony. However, it's now with a difference, because by understanding, you're able to move through this segment and know its meaning.

This card captures the essence of life, not only one life experience, but the total experience. Take the symbolism of this card into your consciousness and meditate on its meaning in your life... here and now. What are you playing... it's your composition and uniquely yours, so look within and follow the daily meditation, which this card imparts, and move deeper into wholeness.

Meditation...

Begin with the morning thoughts:

The Oracle to Freedom

"How long have I continued to live the same lyrics daily, waking in the morning, hearing the same song over and over?

"It's time to reach out... to feel the pulse of my life... to begin to move my consciousness to the end of the composition. For too long I've lost the harmony of my original purpose, but now it's time to play out the final movement... I'm ready to end all desire... all that holds me in this Illusion of my own making.

"As I become aware and feel the greatness, fullness and purpose of my own Being, I desire nothing more than that, because my Personality will bow down to the beauty of the Light which flows from Being.

"In the evening I listen to the songs of the birds, because they complete their life song daily. "Daily I become more attuned with my purpose, because it's my song for the Earth.
"I feel the essence of my song, because it's meant for the Earth, and the Earth receives it through its body to which I'm aligned... as my direct contact with all the Earth's energies.

"As I perceive the beauty which the earth returns to me, and enlivened by the Earth, my symphony never ends because it becomes a part of the Earth's consciousness."

The Oracle to Freedom

Generation

Generations Card

The Oracle to Freedom

You have now selected the Generation card. This card inspires you to reach the ultimate freedom, because it compels you to break free from the shackles of the past. You are now reaching deep into the Earth's consciousness, which forms part of your unconscious, and links the Earth body with your Personality. The combination of these two frequencies, Personality and Earth body, give rise to that state we call "human".

Feel the sense of that binary frequency which allows your Light to move through the Third-dimension to the Earth's innermost essence. Stop now, and compose your mind, and allow the meaning of this card to move your feelings deep within your consciousness and experience the flow of the Earth's consciousness.

The roots of fear are deeply embedded in the generations of Earth-bodies. You know from experience that, although every Earth-body appears separate in your consciousness, and is linked to the Earth, and all the different bodies are antennae which draw Light to the Earth.

Much less has been written and thought about Personality, yet most people feel the Personality represents a frequency in our consciousness which acts as a hindrance in our life experience, one that keeps us separated from One Light. You are so attuned with your Personality that you consider to be you and emphasize this by using the pronoun I.

By drawing the Generation card you are becoming aware that your Personality is responsible for the transmission of consciousness within your body, because it gives purpose and a sense of being to your body. On the down side, your Personality creates stress on the body through interaction between other Personalities.

The Oracle to Freedom

Little is understood regarding the connection that exists between all the human bodies. We think there are individual Personalities in individual bodies, little realizing that relative to the Earth's being and consciousness, all forms and Personalities constitute, and add to the form and Personality of the Earth. There is one Earth and one Personality, and all separation is the result of the Astral Illusion.

Individual Earth-bodies only appear to express separated states of consciousness and this separation is due to the different amount of Light which each body receives. However, all consciousness and all experiences are shared through the generations and their movement through a succession of Earth bodies and Personalities.

When you closely look at the human experience you perceive that most behavior and actions seen in all races are only mechanical which flow from the Earth's unconscious. Variations only occur when stress related situations, such as hardship, grief or illness, temporarily allow more Light to flow through the Personality, and breaks one free from the behavior of generations of experience.

In the present cycle of consciousness there are increasing numbers of Earth bodies' inhabiting the planet. Generally this has become a problem leading to insufficient food supplies and pollution levels in the atmosphere and the environment. These are valid concerns, but many of the religious persuasion believe that there are more "souls" being created, which is a benefit for them.

The Earth is expanding its consciousness at a faster pace, and by creating more bodies, it's attempting to draw more Light, but unfortunately the greater the number of forms, the greater the material destruction of the Earth's organic mantle.

The Oracle to Freedom

As the Earth's consciousness matures it draws the Personality closer to its nature. The Earth depends on all its forms to maintain its basic needs for survival. Should more and more human Personalities turn away from serving the earth's needs, then the Earth achieves this balance by an increase of forms.

Generation is the recurring fields of shared experience passed down or up to succeeding generations. Deep within the DNA fibers of the Earth are the memories of everything that has affected the Earth's consciousness, and these memories are modified by the Personality and the illusory desires created within it.

The Personality was created without desire, however, following its involvement with the Astrals and their Illusion, the Personality desired to be all in ALL, believing it is the soul and the God of man, the ruler of the Earth and its consciousness.

In its desireless state the Personality allowed the Light to manifest for the Earth, because this was the Personality's purpose in creation. However, the Personality became attracted to the sensual passions and began to serve the Earth's nature, and turned away from the Light.

Added to the common behaviors and experiences shared by all humans is the frequency called fear. This, as you have learned, was instilled into the Earth's consciousness by the Astral Lords.

Now you can readily see why many similar events and behaviors of civilization keep recurring, because it all flows from the unconscious of the Earth and is inflamed by the Personality. Over thousands of years certain actions and behaviors in society have become the "agreed" ways of living, and many of these have become enshrined in law. Being

The Oracle to Freedom

"agreed" allows them to continue to flow through consciousness as the normal way to behave. This unconscious agreement manifests as the right to maim, kill and destroy all other creatures. Anything of a lesser importance than humanity are allowed to be wasted, and the killing hasn't stopped with the animals. Since ancient times groups of people have moved migrated to new lands and destroyed all the original inhabitants in order to create the greater race they considered themselves to be. It was common for the invaders to treat the original people as primitives, suggesting they did not possess a soul and relegated them to the status of an animal.

Every new generation believes the older generations have made a mess of life, and rebels, seeking to change the status quo, and instigate a new order of living. The new generation blames the previous generation for all the suffering it appears to be experiencing. Superficially, the new generation dresses differently, creates cute expressions, wears their hair differently, and alter their eating habits believing this is change.

Within the passing of twenty years this generation fall asleep and unconsciously adopt the patterns of their predecessors, following the same rules, the same wars and hand these down to the next generation, who also repeat the same pattern. Because they are Personality driven, they lose their contact with their Light which they experienced at a younger age. The only difference we see with the new generations is that they are forced at an earlier age into the Illusion, and quickly become devoid of their inner contact with their Light Essence.

This is the repetitive cycle within the Earth's consciousness, moving patterns of action and behavior which are only slightly modified by succeeding generations, because all generations are sleep walkers.

The Oracle to Freedom

Personalities engage in the power play, because it understands the latent experiences of the Earth. It uses the illusionary power to manipulate feelings expressed by the Earth and put them into action.

Meditate deep on the imagery of this card, because you have drawn it to increase your awareness and know how you are linked with the Earth's consciousness.

The generations reach back in consciousness to the beginning of the Earth. All who stand in line share the double helix, the bonding of all memory and consciousness.

More subtle are the inherent family ties, which are depicted in old photographs. Often you will unconsciously act and display certain mannerisms, or even share the thoughts and attitudes of a long deceased grandparent, as if they were living in your body.

These old family ties represent the ever-widening layers that surround your body consciousness. They are like various masks that cover your face, and command you to act "out of character" in your present circumstances.

As you peel back the layers you expose your vision to the reality of the generations, and their influence over your behavior.

The old map represents the old world of limitation imposed by the repetitive effect of the generations - one which is a closed view of the world - a world in illusion.

Now you stand at the forefront of many attitudes and feelings, which compose the Earth's consciousness. As you reach out to One Light all these shared emotions and behavior patterns are cast aside, because Light is what the Earth needs now!

Below the hand which peels back the layers are those old body cells each containing the history of the Earth. Each is

The Oracle to Freedom

linked by DNA to the old morphogenetic patterns built into the Earth's by preceding generations.

Now you are aware of the impact which the Earth's consciousness has on your daily life, and now you will separate old behaviors from the present development of your consciousness.

You will sense within when you are behaving like a parent or grandparent, because how often do you unconsciously react as they did, or even speak out words charged with their old emotion and weakness?

This card draws your consciousness to that pivotal point within, that point between your Personality and the Earth, because you will realize that you are still reflecting the old Earth consciousness, one impregnated by the Astral Illusion and passed down through many generations.

Meditation...

As I sit in the quietness of my being I see all the influences of my generations afflicting my thought and behavior.

As I direct my consciousness toward the source of One Light within me I see the mechanical control which I have so willingly allowed in my daily life.

I recognize the beauty and expansiveness of my Being, and realize this body and its Personality are a very small portion of what I truly am.

As I sit here I feel this essence expanding outward, filling this room... filling this dwelling... filling this city. Light is all that is, and my Personality and body are a small part of this. Now I claim

The Oracle to Freedom

One Light, and allow it to encompass all, including my Personality and body, because I love these with the purity of Light.

By changing myself, I change ALL.

The Oracle to Freedom

Freedom

Freedom Card

The Oracle to Freedom

Freedom is an elusive state or condition sought by everyone. Inwardly many people feel trapped, living in circumstances that they believe are not of their making, as something they were born into - an inescapable situation.

Freedom, or the desire for it, is deeply embedded in the human psyche, but it's rarely achieved and experienced.

However, it is the ultimate experience, because to be free is to be pure and untainted, and released from everything that controls and patterns this life experience in the Third-dimension on Earth.

Due to the Personality's fascination with the Astral Illusion, created by the Astral Lords, its direction and desires are directed toward attaining ultimate power, mastery and control over everything that constitutes third dimension. The Personality believes that once all this is achieved, it will be free - free to create and design the conditions of existence favorable for itself, because it will then be God.

Dominating the Personality, the Astral Illusion casts a spell of darkness over the Personality's consciousness. The Astral Entities maintain that deception by controlling most of the information given to humanity by their dominance over the media resources. Much of the information presented attempts to convince people that they are the most advanced beings in the solar system, and that humanity is destined to conquer time and space. This is seen as being the ultimate freedom.

The Astral entities now state that the bio-technological sciences will eliminate all disease in this millennium. All this propaganda builds a prison for humanity, one without walls, which enslaves the mind and consciousness.

Deep within your consciousness you know that the Earth-body is not destined to travel to the stars throughout the

The Oracle to Freedom

universe, because the body is of the earth, and depends on the earth for its sustenance and consciousness. When losing all attachment with the Earth, the body will breakdown and die.

The Personality believes it's imprisoned in the body and it strives within the Astral Illusion to break free. It doesn't realize that its God and the Astral Lords are also imprisoned in another dimension. The Astral Lords know there not and attempt to use force to break down the "walls" of their jail.

At night you look up into the darkness of the sky and direct your attention to the center of the galaxy and beyond. In doing this, you are looking at both the beginning and end of this creation, a creation locked in your concept of time.

This is your prison, because you're trapped by the self-limiting mind set of the Personality. Inwardly you yearn to move your consciousness out into the void of space, but you're unable to do this, because you're locked on the dungeon of self-importance.

The universe and its expanse appear to your consciousness to be there just for you, and you are driven to understand and control it. Why? You don't even have the power to control the Earth, or, for that matter, your own body. How can you possibly understand and control the universe?

This is your limitation and prison, and you seek freedom outside your inner consciousness within the matter of the Third-dimension, and you don't even know what you seek, because your consciousness is trapped within the Astral Illusion.

"I want freedom!" you cry out. Freedom from what?

If you're incapable of recognizing your own prison, how can you seek to escape? Some believe that their present circumstance is their prison, and they move from town to town,

The Oracle to Freedom

country to country, never experiencing anything different other than a change of scenery and culture. Know that your prison is the attitudes within your Personality and not your body, and neither the galaxy nor universe.

The universe is only as large as your consciousness expects it to be.

You look at the stars and they create in your mind a sense of expansiveness, vastness and unknown worlds. Some people claim that for them, the universe is a humbling experience, because they compare its size with the limited size of their body and its ability to move through space and time. Others see the universe as a vast area of space and time inhabited by other life forms, possibly having an advanced technology, and this creates in their mind the elements of fear. No matter what feeling is experienced it's all Personality driven.

What you don't know is that the universe is so small that you can only see it under a powerful microscope, because it's only a speck in Being's consciousness. I the stillness of your own being you can experience the totality of the universe, because everything you gaze at outwardly is contained within the dimension of your body.

More than this, your body is only a minute segment in your total consciousness, because relative to the vastness of your Essence, your body also is the size of dust floating in the atmosphere.

So too your Personality, with its self-love, parades before you its greatness, and it's only as large as a speck of dust relative to the vastness of your being.

Start living in the totality of your consciousness, because this is the way to freedom. Your Personality and the Astral Lords manipulate your mind and consciousness into believing that

The Oracle to Freedom

ultimate freedom will result from moving through the unending circles that constitute and mirror the universe.

There isn't any universe outside your consciousness, because there is only consciousness, only Light. Freedom is experienced through becoming one in Light.

You have drawn the Freedom card and this card incites you to progress toward Inter-dimensional freedom, to experience your Light. Draw your consciousness within so you can expand the Light within. Don't seek outwardly, up or down, or in any direction apart from yourself, because there are no directions in Light. The Light is all encompassing.

Freedom exists within all consciousness, not only human consciousness, because no one part of consciousness is greater than any other form. The same consciousness flows through the lion; horse, dog, and in fact, through all creatures and plants within the Earth's body. The only difference is the quantity not the quality. When you assume that your consciousness is greater than anything else, you have no freedom, because this assumption is your prison, one of your many cocoons.

You have to understand that there's nothing that exists beyond your consciousness, because you are your consciousness at your particular level. You marvel at the brightness of the night sky, and enjoy the warmth of the Sun during the day. Are you bound to the Earth? No matter what you think, when you close your eyes, you exist in a vast universe of consciousness, one that is greater than all the galaxies in the universe, because they only mirror a small part of Being's consciousness.

Conceptually you are locked in many cocoons built up over many life recurrences and they are all awaiting opening. These cocoons represent those fears, lies, and grabs for power, which you've locked within yourself.

The Oracle to Freedom

Like the butterfly you emerge from, and leave all the shells of your recurrent lives scattered beneath you. You spread your wings of freedom, revealing a body of Light and beauty, free from the limitations of the old cocoons and now expressing your consciousness, Love and Light for all to see and enjoy.

Your body isn't your cocoon, although you think it is. Your cocoon is your Personality and its fixation on the astral Illusion.

Break free from this dimensional prison and spread your wings of Light, and from deep within express the totality of your being, one which transverses all dimensions, because you are FREE, NOW and FOREVER.

Meditation...

By selecting this card I'm moving my consciousness into the Light of my Essence.

I'm breaking free from this self-made prison of the Astral Illusion, one which the Personality has woven around my consciousness.

As I recognize the vastness of my being as what transverses all dimensions, I truly express Light which engulfs the cocoon, warms it, and melts the outer coating to reveal the true Light.

As the Light of my being spreads throughout this dimension, I see I'm not what the world consciousness implies I am.

I needn't know whether the world is flat or round, or whether the universe is a great expanse of galaxies, which are to be

The Oracle to Freedom

conquered and controlled. I haven't any need for this Astral Illusion, because I'm already free.

I no longer listen to the ignorance and darkness of human consciousness dominated by the Astral Illusion through my Personality, because I know that within the smallest speck of dust floating in the air there exists all the consciousness of Self.

I'm free and I spread my wings of Light and shine forth in the ever present moment of Light. I'm free to be what I AM - One Light.

The Oracle to Freedom

The Oracle to Freedom

Fear

Fear Card

The Oracle to Freedom

Look deeply into the depths of this card, because there is no simplicity in fear.

Within the Astral Illusion there are many faces, some hidden, others contorted; hollow eyes looking out - warning. Those are the eyes of the Astral Illusion, always watching, always fearing what others will do or think.

You stand strong in the face of fear. You feel that by closing your eyes nothing exists - that nothing will harm you - and you're safe from everything that happens around you. Inwardly, you know you can't hide from what you created in your life, and in time, like rotting garbage, it begins to disintegrate, and your hardened countenance begins to crack. Non-involvement doesn't protect you from the fear that it may also happen to you.

You look back at the hardened image you created, an image petrified with fear, which is lost in the Astral Illusion, not feeling, but decaying in the flow of nothing - a frequency of disintegration. It's lost the art of integrating with the frequencies of love and joy.

When you look back you begin to lose touch with what you truly are, because you're becoming identified with a cold statue frozen in fear, the hands that reach out to touch you can't penetrate the web of illusion which hides your face.

Thousands of eyes watch you, drawing you into their frequencies, because those caught in fear are not alone, and they want to draw you into their realm, They exist below your waking consciousness.

Why have you drawn this card?

It's to direct your attention to see those fears that haunt your consciousness, because you agreed to accept these fears, and now, in this moment, they demand your attention. You have to face their demands, because they seek to destroy your Light.

The Oracle to Freedom

It's said that the night has a thousand eyes, but within the darkness of your sensual being there are many more watching, flowing from many previous life recurrences, still seeking their ultimate outcome, because they too, have journeyed with you to this point in consciousness.

Open your inner eyes and see what you are. Accept those eyes you were, and by relating them to what you are now, you'll be free from their control.

Know that these eyes are phantoms of your life recurrences, which you've accepted by following your Personality's involvement in the Astral Illusion.

Touch your real feelings and experience the truth of your being, which is One Light, because in Light there is no fear.

This card reminds you that you still live in fear; otherwise you wouldn't have drawn it. So don't throw it aside, because to do so means that you will draw it time and time again until you clear your consciousness of all fear.

Know also that this fear dwells deep in your consciousness, and it's only your Personality that falsely tells you that now you no longer live in fear.

Heed well its meaning and take this card now, because you've inwardly selected it. It beckons you to look more deeply into your life and consciousness.

Open your eyes and look deeply into all those accusing eyes around you, all those eyes that condemn you and blame you for creating them.

You're blameless, so release those phantoms from your consciousness and become free of them.

Remember, fear only exists in your Personality and is reflected through your body. The earth has no fear, and only your Personality lives in fear and the pain associated with it.

The Oracle to Freedom

This is your card of the moment. Take it and use it in your meditation.

Don't allow the Astral Illusion and your Personality to suggest that the frequencies of fear no longer exist within you. When you are One Light you will then have no fear.

Meditation...

Love softens my consciousness, because it gives warmth and security. It softens the demands of Personality and turns the Personality's face away from the Astral Illusion. The warmth of Love moves through my Personality dispersing and consuming all fear, allowing me to express Light and Love through this body.

With this Love there is no fear, because fear only exists in the Astral Illusion, and I no longer exist in this Illusion.

I no longer close my eyes to the warmth of Love and Light flowing through my Personality from the source of all Light.

I'm touched by all this Light and Lover which exists in the now, and direct my gaze no longer to the Astral Illusion and its coldness.

Such coldness only represents repression, hate and delusion.

I have drawn this card, because unless I face these masks of many life recurrences, the fears which I have embedded in my consciousness will chain me to this dimension and illusion.

The Oracle to Freedom

I AM LIGHT-N I AM LOVE! And because I express the warmth and Light, I am Light, and within Light there's no fear.

The Oracle to Freedom

Astral Illusion

Astral Illusion Card

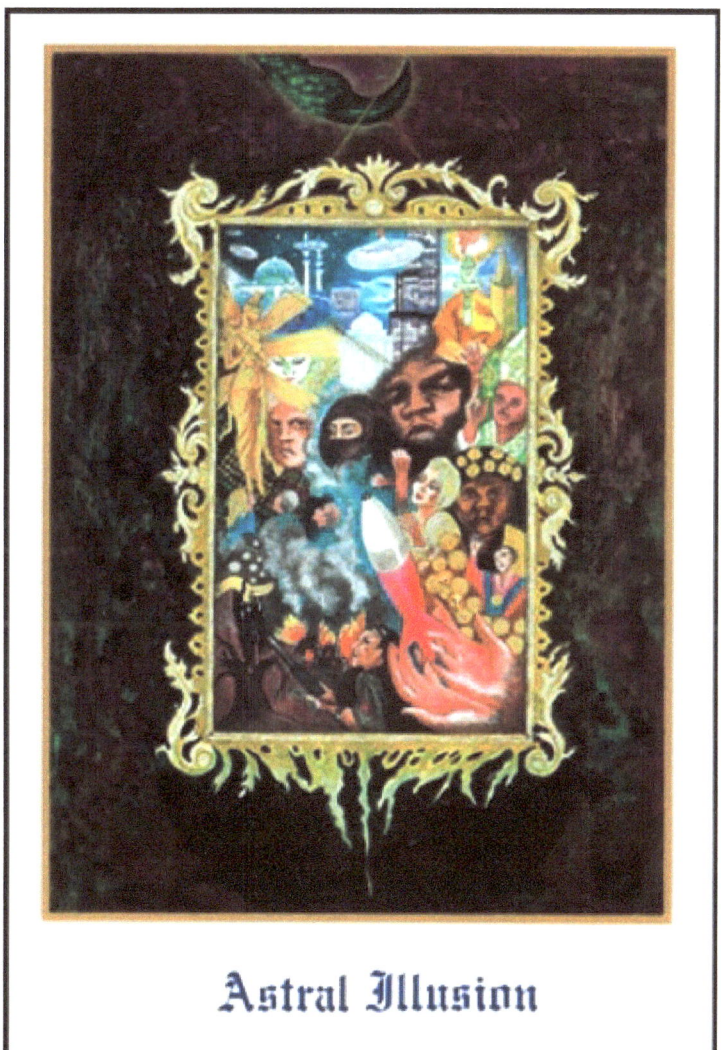

The Oracle to Freedom

All the world's a stage, and you're the central actor in this play of life.

They say the world is an illusion, but you love this illusion, because although within it there's an element of danger, the illusion is what grounds you to living this life.

You love the stability, the sense of reality; because you're unable to reach out and touch it, and know that you are of sane mind.

Everyone who you live and work with experience the same reality picture, and that's your comfort, and there are always those authorities there to protect you from harm.

Everything you see, feel, taste, hear and smell represents your reality of life, and when any of these receptors are denied you, you seem to die a little.

You accept the need to destroy the forests, because you need to indiscriminately waste paper. You love to belong to a great and powerful nation that is ever ready to put down the dictators of smaller nations.

There are the golden icons of the different faiths and religions which provide the peace and security knowing that you will have an assured future following your body's death. There are secret societies dedicated to teaching you how to gain personal power in order that you can bridge the gap of infinity and attain the ultimate secrets of life, which include power and immortality. Only the Astral Illusion can grant such power to everyone considered worthy to receive it.

There are those who live by the gun and get their just deserts. On the other side, there are the great humanitarians who lead the minds of men and women into greater awareness of the need to work together in one purpose to enhance life.

Great edifices are built by businesses, governments and

churches which demonstrate their wealth and power so that they can dupe the mass of humanity into the belief that by supporting them, they will receive assistance and [protection in times of need. All thought and action within the Astral Illusion is directed toward a give and take situation. There's always a balance of wealth and power, because when it's lost by one person, it's taken up by others. This tends to hold the mass of humanity in bondage, allowing individuals to amass personal fortunes.

And what better way to strengthen the Astral Illusion than to create a conspiracy? Conspiracies allow those in power to control and influence those dissidents who seem to undermine the status quo.

Many people expect there will be an alien invasion, or this has already happened. When society begins to break down, and governments get out of control, and the religious sects no longer are able to promote moral and spiritual stability, the threat of an alien invasion is considered as the only course that will set things right. Most people are bound to the Astral Illusion and as such, prefer to have some authority that thinks for them and protect them from each other.

If it's not aliens who have the answer to all this confusion in the world, then other people believe that change will occur by the visitation of a great God who will descend from heaven and destroy all the heathens and set up a beautiful Illusion on earth for all the faithful.

That, beloved Light Being, is the expression of the great mirror depicted on this card, one that reflects the mood and consciousness of humanity, because the mirror is suspended on the claw of the Astrals as their symbol of power and control. It's held together by an ornate frame, one which depicts its importance and brilliance. However, it hangs in front of a murky background, which is the darkness of the Astral Lords consciousness, projected through the mirror into this dimension.

By drawing this card you should question your relationship to your life in this Astral Illusion.'

How do you react to all the negative reports published in your daily newspaper and television broadcasts? Are you constantly living in fear of what may be the outcomes? Will your savings become worthless when the illusory stock market is manipulated by the power struggles of the Astral Entities? By denying the needs of one country, the Astral Entities create civil wars so that one country's loss is another's gain.

Because it's only an Illusion, there are no winners or losers, because the Astral Illusion is the means where the Astral Lords drawer their greatest energy from humanity's suffering. They have no care for the planet, and their Illusion is firmly built into a Time Loop where all civilization is systematically built up and destroyed in planned cycles. They move human consciousness along a well planned and trodden path where they create the situation for the re-experience of the same destitute life cycle.

Anyone who has seen the Astral Illusion for what it truly is will say, "There's nothing new under the Sun." The Astral Illusion repeats its flow of discovery and technology which the mind of humanity sees as a growing achievement. However, what isn't seen is that there is very little change in human emotions and behavior, because these are all determined by the Astral Illusion. Humanity still react and behave the same way they did some eighty thousand years ago. You have to realize that the so- called technology of the Astral Illusion controls the laws that dominate human consciousness, producing no growth in understanding and behavior. It can be said that you can change your clothes and hairstyle, but you don't change your inner response.

To break free from the Astral Illusion you have to remember, not the passing of the Time Loop, but your own being. You are the true Light and not your Personality, which struggles to live on the top of the heap, so you have to break free of the bonds that hold you a prisoner.

While the Astral Entities hold before you the mirror of the Illusion, and often suggest you can live a great life in spirit by following the paths of the great avatars who periodical appeared on earth, these Entities continually hinder your progress by insisting their Illusion can only be experienced when you follow a system of their making, under the auspices of a great teacher.

This is the ultimate power of the Astral Illusion, because by directing everything away from you to an outward authority, you will never look within. The external focus of your thought and action is directed to the Astral Illusion, keeping you subservient to its purpose.

Understand that the Astral Illusion is only a mirror which is powerless to control you unless you give it the power to do so.

Meditation...

All that surrounds me is only a reflection of my own making.

I no longer have my Personality reflect the false concepts of the Illusion, because to deny the existence of the Illusion is the first coming of Light into my earthly consciousness.

The Oracle to Freedom

The Ego is a lens, one that either magnifies the Illusion or magnifies the Light.

For too long now I've accepted the mirrored images of death and destruction, hate and greed. I no longer seek to have these destructive frequencies occupying my consciousness.

As the first rays of Light illuminate my consciousness, I sense the power of that Light, which is full of warmth and love.

It fills my consciousness and there is no room for anything else.

As I allow the Light to flood my consciousness every second of my life, I need nothing, because I am all.

The Oracle to Freedom

Healing the Earth

Healing the Earth Card

The Oracle to Freedom

Healing is something that belongs to the human consciousness, and it is linked to feelings of pain, depression, loneliness or any other condition that stems from the Illusion, which creates separation from the inner consciousness of Essence.

People usually link healing with health, which is incorrect. Health represents an original state, such as a perfect pattern, and when this pattern becomes altered we say that this change in functioning is a disease. The process involved in returning something to its original pattern is called healing. As such, healing is an invisible force or frequency that seeks to return something to its wholeness. Healing is the integration of Oneness, and for humanity it reflects the return to One Light.

However, healing isn't limited to the human experience, because it exists throughout the universe and Being, where everything moves outward from its source and returns to fulfilment and completion.

Until you complete your inner healing you won't begin the healing for the Earth.

Your Personality has separated your Essence from contact with the Earth, and then fragmented the Earth's consciousness. The Earth's consciousness is projected through all its forms, and when the Personality denied the Earth the Light and consciousness of Self, it caused the seeds of disease and destruction to occur.

You are responsible for the Earth, and primarily your body, because it's your connection to the Earth and is the Earth.

Feel within your heart that the Earth, and all its expression of consciousness through its nature, represents the sum of its parts, which express the whole consciousness of the Earth.

The Earth needs to be whole because it's purpose is to

The Oracle to Freedom

become one with its source, the Sun.

Many people have little regard for the Earth, and consider it's a rock floating in space, devoid of any feeling or consciousness. Others embrace the philosophy that the Earth is a living organism, one that expresses life throughout the organic matter that composes its surface mantle, which only goes part of the way in knowing the Earth's true nature, because the Earth's is total and not limited to one part.

There are people who are totally controlled by the Astrals and their Illusion who believe the Earth has negative emotions, such as, revenge, hate and destructive tendencies that are directed solely toward humanity, little knowing that when the Earth makes adjustments to its organism which is outwardly reflected as volcanic eruptions, floods, wild fires and drought, the Earth is punishing humanity for their misdeeds.

As a complete organism, the Earth has no tendencies to act like a God of the Old Testament, who punishes everyone who transgresses his laws and decrees. Many of the Earth changes are the result of climate changes that are directly influenced by solar variations. Generally, we experience changes outside our conscious control with our body, and we don't attribute these changes to supernatural forces.

You have drawn this card to be reminded that you must take responsibility for the Earth, and to initiate the healing process through healing your body on all levels of consciousness.

This is a grey and destructive area in consciousness where humans exist, because it results from self- interest and greed, where no Light flows for healing. Unfortunately even though the greed is limited to a few individuals, it's supported by the mass of people who are also guilty of the destructive process.

As forests are laid bare, not for housing, but for profit and

The Oracle to Freedom

greed, plants die creating deserts where forests once flourished. It doesn't end there, because all the homes and habitats of the animals, birds and insects are gone forever, including the species that once lived there.

Like an ostrich you place your head in the sand and pretend that it doesn't matter. But soon the lack of trees and creatures limit the consciousness available for the earth, as well as your health and wellbeing, which increases the Astral dominance over the dimensional consciousness.

As you see on this card, there is a point where the green touches the barren grayness where small plants struggle to survive.

Become aware of your environment and see how the Earth strives to heal itself from the human induced destruction.

Move your consciousness into harmony with the green plant shoots, and assist in the healing, which expands and uniting the consciousness of the forests, rivers and waterfalls creating the rainbow, which is the bridge joining healing with wholeness.

The Earth spirits, the Elementals, coordinate their Light to rebuild the morphogenetic patterns of the Earth, its trees and waterways, nourishing their being and increasing the consciousness in preparation of the new born child, the Earth child, whose Light and consciousness no longer allows the destructive attempts of the Illusional Personalities to serve the Astral purpose.

All power and healing lies within the rebirth of the Earth's consciousness, and you alone are responsible for the healing. You can't tell others they should do something, because all responsibility lies with the individual. When you heal the Earth, you will also heal your self.

Once you've removed all the seeds of disease from your

The Oracle to Freedom

consciousness and no longer project them into your body, the earth the Earth will be regenerated.

As your awareness and behavior influences others they will become more conscious of the Earth and its needs. By giving to the earth through your body, you create a synergistic pattern which links all energies in the Earth's consciousness.

Now unleash the healing energies within your own being and precipitate the healing frequencies within all, drawing everything into the oneness of Light.

Feel the thrill of this change developing within your frequency, a change which produces clarity of mind and love for everything, and return to the Oneness in Light.

Meditation...

Deep within my consciousness I feel the long connection which I've experienced with this beautiful Earth, the home of this body, and many others which I've been connected with over thousands of years.

I've forgotten to love this Earth Being, and I remembering, I remember my true self, moving Light into the growing Earth consciousness.

As I contemplate this card I feel my awareness expand and know that I too have been guilty of creating barrenness on this planet, and the destruction of life and energy, because by engaging in this destruction, I also destroy a part of my body.

Open me to my Light.

Let it shine throughout the nature of the Earth, and into my body. Create a beautiful rainbow, because it's my bridge to Light.

Turn away from all Illusion, Personality of mine.

Allow the Light Child to flow through to my body and the earth.

Allow the healing to flow, as the Earth becomes whole and free from the Astral Illusion.

Balanced Personality

Balanced Personality Card

The Oracle to Freedom

Now draw together all the forces of your being into complete harmony, because this is the card of perfect balance. Your journey begins and ends here, because completeness is the full circle.

There is no beginning or end, because you always were and are! You are Light and as such, are always complete within the heart of all. Now experience the circle of Light.

In the stillness of your being, your consciousness acts as a fulcrum for all the Light that flows to and through you.

This is the moment where you exist in the timeless state of Being, because here you experience the blending of the primal forces underlying all creation, that of the Light.

Move deep within the stillness of your own consciousness and stop all inner talking, and blend the colors of the two major forces if your consciousness, the intellect and feeling, and complete the circle of perfection.

Ponder the beauty of the Light and allow your Personality ton witness again the glory of infinite Light as it bathes your consciousness with pure thought and warm love, because it's the underlying nature of your being. Savor this moment.

Begin your movement into Light and completeness by feeling the beauty of the earth, because it too is a being of Light like you.

As a summer's day comes to a close, the brilliant light of the Sun bathes the earth from its heavenly position in the western sky.

It's the summer solstice, and the Earth receives the warmest caresses from its loving partner, because it receives its warmth and love from a greater Light.

And the earth responds to this loving wave of Light, expressing its pleasure in beautiful colors where the whole landscape comes alive.

Listen to the sounds of Nature at dusk, the birds and insects calling forth the night and peace.

The trees stand calm as the breezes of the hot day calm to a gentle movement, because all awaits the night and the bright stars in the heaven.

Stand and allow your inner nature to experience this moment in consciousness as the outer nature of the universe reflects the glory within you. The bright orb of Light in the western sky reflects the fullness of the Light within you, which after the darkness, returns in the morning to illuminate all.

It's time for your illumination, because this is your ultimate desire, to be bathed in the Light of creation.

Feel the peace and warmth within your breast as the Light illuminates your consciousness and you reflect the beauty and colors of your nature.

By drawing this card you are awakening the pulse of life, one that beckons you to complete the circle, and bring the Personality to focus once again on its Light source, so that you will always live in complete illumination.

There is no reasoning with this card, because its message is one of inner feeling and desire; that of balancing these two states to complete the circle and the opening of your Personality to reflect all.

Throughout thousands of years how many people have sought the Philosophers Stone, the pearl within each one of us? And also, how many others have closeted themselves in monasteries, or in mountain caves, seeking the experience of total consciousness and oneness, only to fail?

Those few who balanced their Personality experienced to a greater or lesser extent oneness with their creator. This experience is a feeling of oneness with Nature, the universe and Being, and now it's here for you.

By practising these meditations daily, and allowing the energies of your being to permeate your consciousness, the memory returns, and as the extended circles draw closer together in your consciousness, you experience the Light of your being, not only now, but forever. You now have the keys to truth and freedom. Take them and open the circle of Light to flow.

All you have to do is ALLOW - allow the Personality to blend with the feeling element of its nature and complete the circle of the universe.

This will change your life and consciousness forever, because it's what you are and have always been, and it's the experience for all humanity and the Earth.

Meditation...

I move through the frequencies of consciousness as the bee moves from flower to flower. There now seems to be more flowers for my consciousness, for me to taste the nectar.

I love the warmth of the Sun as it maintains the power and strength of all the cells of my body. I'm nourished by the energies my blood receives from the Sun.

I love the peace and harmony of all Nature, all that works together to maintain this living planet which moves gracefully and harmoniously around the great orb of Light, accepting its Light and loving its warmth, which expands its Light and Love.

The Oracle to Freedom

Now as I close my eyes, I move through the black pupil of the eye which I see in my consciousness, which opens to the Light and Oneness of All, because in this moment in Being, I experience the totality of Being. There is no mystery, because all is one in simplicity.

If you prefer to have the actual Oracle Cards, they can be purchased separately on our website to accompany this book.

Please visit http://www.LightPulsations.com

The Oracle to Freedom

For further information email us at
lightpulsations@gmail.com

Read our other titles for inspiration and upliftment, and a greater understanding of Zadore's message of Light.

Books by JON WHISTLER:
   ONE LIGHT
   THE EARTH LIGHT TRANSMISSIONS
   THE VOLAH TRANSMISSIONS,
   SERIES ONE TO THREE

Books by SIZZOND ZADORE:
   ENTER THE VORTEX AS ONE LIGHT

Books by AN EMISSARY OF VOLAH:
   VIS NOVAE NATURA
   GUIDANCE ON THE WAY 1 and 2

Visit our website: http://www.lightpulsations.com

The Oracle to Freedom

The Oracle to Freedom

The Oracle to Freedom

www.ingramcontent.com/pod-product-compliance
Lightning Source LLC
Chambersburg PA
CBHW042326150426
43193CB00001B/6